Simple Happy

Simple Happy

◆

Finally Learning
to Listen to Yourself

Andy Feld

iUniverse, Inc.
New York Lincoln Shanghai

Simple Happy
Finally Learning to Listen to Yourself

iUniverse books may be ordered through booksellers or by contacting:

iUniverse
2021 Pine Lake Road, Suite 100
Lincoln, NE 68512
www.iuniverse.com
1-800-Authors (1-800-288-4677)

Because of the dynamic nature of the Internet, any Web addresses or links contained in this book may have changed since publication and may no longer be valid.

The views expressed in this work are solely those of the author and do not necessarily reflect the views of the publisher, and the publisher hereby disclaims any responsibility for them.

Cover photos by ABC Music Video & Photography (www.abc-mvp.com)

Design and layout by Tom Hastings

ISBN: 978-0-595-43626-2 (pbk)
ISBN: 978-0-595-87951-9 (ebk)

Printed in the United States of America

You should not be afraid to admit that enjoyment of life is your number one goal.

This short, simple book is, in essence, a handbook for our day-to-day happiness. A fast-paced, easy read, "Simple Happy" moves from one life topic to the next, giving the reader a multitude of choices on how to increase their enjoyment. From "Why am I here?" to "Where am I going?" to "How am I getting there?," the perspective is new and thought-provoking. Find a quiet corner, sit down for a while, and relax into this book's simple pleasures.

Dedicated to Mom, Dad, Jon, Mike, and Dyanna, but most of all, Julie, whose relentless love and encouragement led me to write this book.

Many thanks to Carol, my long-time assistant, who somehow managed to decipher my handwritten scribbles and convert them into readable print.

My thanks, as well, to my proofreader/editor, Judith Myers, who cleaned up my act.

Contents

Simple Happy

Preface

The content of this book has been swirling around in my head for over twenty years. I always knew I wanted to share my thoughts but, as you know, the idea of sitting down to "write a book" can be daunting. So, why did I finally take the plunge?

If there is anything I am sure of, it is that the more you explain and teach a subject, the more insight into that subject you, yourself, acquire. I have experienced this over and over again throughout my adult life. Every time I teach salespeople about selling, I become better at sales. Every time I teach someone how to ski better, I become a better skier. The fact is, teaching and explaining increase learning. I love getting smarter about things which are important to me.

For me, the most important goal in life is to be happy as much of the time as possible. Truthfully, it is more important than anything else, and that includes family, friends and business. The more I can successfully share that premise with you, the reader, the more I, too, will learn and thus benefit from it.

The inspiration to finally sit down and write this book came at an unexpected moment. On the 7th of August, 2005, in Tanzania, Africa, I was climbing the legendary Mt. Kilimanjaro; certainly not a technically demanding trek, but physically challenging, to say the least. I am an avid hiker, and climbing Kilimanjaro had long been the goal of my friends, lead by Kenny, and of my wife and me. On Sunday, August,

6th, we set out on our six-day trek from the Machame gate in Tanzania. At the end of the second day, when we made camp at the Shira hut, it happened!

What creates inspiration is difficult to comprehend and explain. For me, it was a combination of the following: Altitude of 12,300 ft., views looking down on a sea of clouds covering the rainforest below, and a magnificent sunset. (Living in the high desert of Albuquerque, New Mexico, and watching the sun set over our west mesa had made me a sunset expert.) We were enjoying a beautiful interaction with twenty-three local Tanzanian guides and porters, and I was experiencing a star-lit evening the like of which I had never seen before. Call it whatever you want: beauty, love, peace, warmth … Just know that, then and there, I decided it was finally time to start writing.

By that time, I had accumulated twenty years of my handwritten notes from numerous sources about 'life,' all of which I had stored in a folder. These were little tidbits I had picked up from reading, listening to tapes, and simple life experience. I returned from Africa, opened the folder, spread out the notes and began to organize my thoughts to write this book.

I am certain I have benefited from this exercise, and I sincerely hope the same will be true for you. Enjoy.

Why Me?

So, what qualifies me to write this book? That's a good question, and my only answer is that I have lived a relatively normal life, just like you. I grew up comfortable middle class in New Jersey, with what I would consider life's normal ups and downs. At age six, I was in the hospital for almost two months with a blood clot which required two surgeries. My Little League baseball career ranged from being the last-picked right fielder at age ten to being an All Star at age twelve, and then the ultimate devastation of being cut from my high school baseball team in the tenth grade. I was a mediocre student and socially middle of the pack. I'm now fifty-four years of age and my primary life goal for the past twenty years has been to be as happy as I can possibly be in the current moment.

My life experiences are not unusual. After leaving New Jersey, I graduated from Denver University, stayed in Colorado for eleven years, and then moved to Albuquerque, New Mexico, for the next twenty-five years. I have been married, divorced and re-married. I have two grown children and have raised numerous happy dogs. I have had business successes as well as disappointments. I cannot point to any one defining, life-changing experience. However, some time in the late 1980's, I started to seriously question "the purpose of life for me." I was, at the time, approaching forty years of age, had two young children, was in a deteriorating marriage, and was going through a business failure. I was feeling more and more unhappy and even somewhat of a victim. For me, it was time to ask some life questions. I started searching for answers, and they started coming from all directions: from people, books, and series of tapes. I decided, then, that being happy <u>now</u> was Priority Number One, and I have dedicated a good deal of time to achieving just that.

What has worked for me may not all work for you in every way. We are each different. Read the book. Absorb what feels good and discard the rest. If unsure about something, try it on for a while and see how it feels. Learn to trust your feelings. Much of what I have written may raise more questions than answers for you. This is good!

It is said that when the student is ready, the teacher will arrive. Ask the questions. When I was ready, the teachers came from everywhere. They will for you, as well. If the timing is right for you and me, how wonderful! Let us begin.

Why Are We

Here?

Who has not asked themselves these questions, many times? *Who am I? What am I? Why now?* The list of questions goes on forever. Just like you, my quest for "Simple Happy" started with these very same questions. I love direct, simple answers. Try this one!

WE ARE HERE TO EXPERIENCE THE UNIQUENESS OF OUR HUMAN LIFE WITH AS MUCH JOY IN THE PRESENT MOMENT AS POSSIBLE.

Each of our life experiences is incredibly far-reaching, but unique to us individually. We all have ups and downs, victories and defeats. It is what life experience is: learning to experience "Life" with as much joy as possible. That is my ultimate goal.

From this point on, in the book, everything mentioned is designed to accomplish the above statement. If you agree with my statement, then we are off to a good start.

I am not here (on Earth, right now, in this body) to change the world, to make my children better, to be responsible for others' happiness, to accomplish any certain tasks, etc. I am here, first and foremost, to enjoy the moment as much as possible.

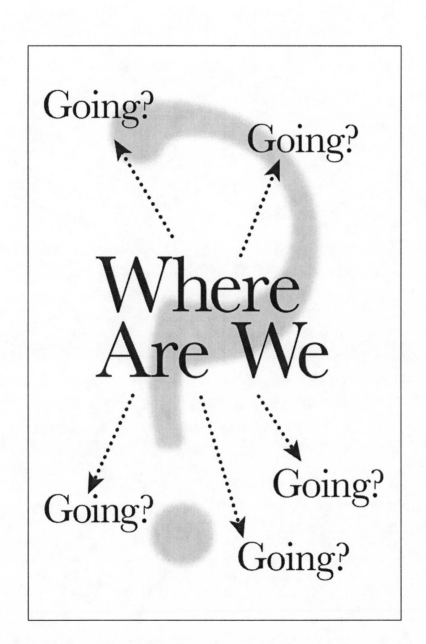

Are you heading in the direction you desire, or do you feel as if life is just dragging you along?

In life, do we create our daily experience, or is the grand design all laid out for us?

I have come to know, with good awareness and certainty, that each of us has the ability to create our individual experience here on Earth. How wonderful a thought! Think about it. We actually have the ability to create our moment, our day, and our life.

So, how is this actually possible? Very simply, it is through our thoughts. About twenty years ago, when I started questioning everything, I came across a motivational tape series by Dr. Denis Waitley. As with most pieces of this kind, I would listen and absorb the entire series, but usually walk away with only one or two new ideas to try to incorporate into my life. In this particular instance, I walked away with one enormous new concept. I may not be quoting Dr. Waitley exactly, but his message was, 'You always move in the direction of your current, most dominant thoughts.' This statement has turned out to be not only a great realization, but a good foundation for where and how I want to direct my life experience.

What a powerful statement! If we move in the direction of our current, most dominant thoughts, and if, as human beings, we have the ability to control our thoughts, then there are no limits to where we can go. WOW!

A recent movie, "What the?#!#? Do We Know Anyway?," attempts to explain this whole thought-reality process through quantum physics. For those of you who require scientific proof, try this movie. So, what are your current, most dominant thoughts? Are they filled with negativity, i.e.: "I really dislike my job," "I really attract bad relationships," "I hate my body," "The political agenda of our leaders keeps me from getting what I really want," "Why is my physical health poor?," "I never have any money," etc.? Do you regularly participate in pity parties with your friends, constantly reminding each other of all the woes of the world and yourselves?

Or are your most dominant thoughts those of joyous anticipation of what might be: "I can't wait for that perfect relationship," "That new job I'm searching for will be so wonderful," "This diet and exercise is great," "The sunsets here are so beautiful," etc.?

Come to grips with it, right now!! WHATEVER YOUR CURRENT, MOST DOMINANT THOUGHTS ARE, THAT IS THE DIRECTION IN WHICH YOU ARE HEADING. If you want to change your path, then change your thoughts. Do it RIGHT NOW! Steven Covey, in his *Seven Habits* book, speaks of the unique ability human beings have to control their actions by thinking first. Why not start by giving it a try?

Later in this book, I will present a step-by-step approach to changing your thoughts and learning to manifest just what you want.

Look in the Mirror

- You
are
Responsible

Everything that is going on in your life is created by you, so you are responsible for it all. I know this is not always easy to hear, but it is the basis for actually getting what you do want. Every time you say something like, "Just my luck," or "Murphy's law," or "I'm always in the 5% who gets the medical reaction," etc., you are denying your responsibility for your own life.

In the mid-1980's, as all these thoughts and questions about life were coming at me, I was introduced to the wonderful little book entitled "Napkin Notes on the Art of Living" by G. Michael Durst, Ph.D. The simplicity (I love simple things) of his book, along with its direct message of total responsibility, jolted me like never before.

I realized, then and there, that my ENTIRE life experience was MY responsibility. How novel a thought! It is not my boss's fault. It is not my wife's fault. It is not the other driver's fault. It is not the guy-next-door's fault. I AM RESPONSIBLE FOR MY LIFE!

We all try really hard to figure out why our daily events are not our responsibility. You know, "If my taxes were not so high," or "If my landlord would only….," or "If the street signs were better," or "If the fast-food places wouldn't put in fat," etc.

GET OVER IT!

I know it may not be easy, but right now, look in the mirror and see who is responsible for creating your life.

Often, early in my life, when business pursuits were not going well for me, I had a regular tendency to injure my lower back. Sound familiar? Oh, poor me. If it wasn't for my bad back, I could go out and fix the problem, but, darn that back! Sound familiar?

I finally figured out that both my business problems and my back problems were totally my responsibility to fix. With this realization, I was empowered to turn things around, and I did it by changing my thoughts. This is usually not an over-night process, and certainly changing your thoughts 180 degrees is downright difficult, if not impossible. It is a process, and it starts with small thought changes, right now, which in turn lead to big thought changes, over time. Today, I have fewer back problems in my fifties than I did when I was in my thirties. Taking responsibility released my fears!

It is an accepted reality in several circles of healing that emotions affect physical well-being. The old saying, "What a pain in the neck," is expressed frequently. The expression reflects that stubbornness or inflexibility can truly cause a painful neck.

When looking in the mirror, decide to take responsibility and feel the self-empowerment. Experience that 'Simple Happy' SMILE.

Opposites

Attract?

Not!

In order to understand and create personal change, it is critical that we understand what attracts us to anything.

We have all heard that opposites attract, and from some scientific points of view, it may be accurate. My experience in day-to-day life says that this is simply not the case. The fact is, I find that similar ideas, thoughts and feelings, shared with other people, are almost always what draw us together. Differences in these areas create dissension or even repel us. Are people, countries, organizations, and religions drawn together by similarities or differences? Are your friends and social groups made up of people who see the world somewhat as you do or unlike you? Are your favorite relationships with those who are like you or unlike you? In almost all cases, it is similarities that attract, not opposites. This is one of the most important concepts of my book, so let us go further.

Our entire life revolves around the attraction of similarities. We cannot attract anything we want if we are dissimilar. How do we tell when we are similar to something or someone? Easy! We feel good and happy about that something or someone. Do not make it any more difficult than that. If you feel happy and good about something or someone, you have the ability to attract it.

For a moment, think of that FEELING you get when you are attracted to a person, an event, or a course of action. It is because you FEEL similarly: happy and content with that person, that event or course of action. Your level of happiness is the way to measure your similarity to something. If the thought of a person, event or action makes you feel good (happy), you have the similarities needed for attracting what you want.

I want to make this as simple as possible. If you want more money but you dislike or hate money, your chance to attract it is nil. If you want a new, wonderful relationship but your thoughts about relationships are scary and negative, then you cannot attract the relationship you say you desire. If you want to become strong and healthy but you are jealous of strong, healthy people, you do not have the similarities needed to attract strength and health.

We must focus on what we want by putting all of our attention toward the positives of our desires, rather than the negatives associated with not having what we want.

If you want a new job, is the majority of your attention focused on the new, wonderful job you want, or are you focusing on the lousy boring job you have? Your point of emotional focus dictates whether you are a match to what you want.

Getting What You

You

Want:

The Emotional Match

Is there anything more important than getting what we want, right now? Getting the job, getting the project done, being healthy, attracting the right relationship, planning the perfect vacation, lowering the golf score, owning the perfect car, etc., etc., etc. The list may not be endless, but I assure you that as soon as you get something you really want, a new desire will appear! It always does.

Before I continue, let's review some of the points we have already considered in previous chapters, and hopefully agree on some basics. First, whatever you are thinking about, regardless of what you want, is where you are headed. For instance, if you really want that new house, what are your thoughts? Are you jealous of the people who already have it? Are you depressed about your current living situation? Do you worry about your lack of money keeping you from the house? IF THESE ARE YOUR MOST DOMINANT THOUGHTS, you are not moving toward your dream house. However, do you fantasize about driving through the new neighborhood? Do you see yourself mowing the lawn of this house? Most of all, does the thought of achieving this dream house make you feel invigorated and alive? If your most dominant thoughts are of the wonderful aspects of this house, you are moving towards what you want. If not, you are stalled.

Next, who is responsible for getting this house for you? Is it your spouse, the lottery, your boss giving you a raise, the government making it easier to buy homes, or are YOU, yes, YOU responsible? Take total responsibility.

So, we now agree, your dominant thoughts are in the right place, and you are totally responsible for getting the house: Right? Great! You are now empowered.

For most of my adult life, I believed the road map to getting what you wanted was 1) setting the goal; 2) Making the action plan to achieve the goal; and 3) working like crazy to carry out the plan. I still believe that Steps 1, 2 and 3, along with the proper thoughts and self-responsibility, will get you most of what you want. However, over the past five years, I have learned the all-important Step 4, which dramatically speeds up the process. Remember, in last chapter, we said similarities attract? That is the key to Step 4: <u>You must be an emotionally similar match to what it is you want.</u> Stay with me, and I'll explain!

<u>Number 1: Setting the Goal:</u> What is it you want? Don't just write it down, be as specific as you possibly can. Here's a quick example: My wife and I have lived a similar timeline. We are close in age. We each married for the first time when we were young. We each had twenty-year first marriages. We each had two children. After divorce, we were each single for approximately five years. I need to add that we had never met each other before. After enjoying the new-found freedoms of being single, we independently decided that life with a partner would be best for each of us. Interestingly enough, in setting the goal of finding a new partner, each of us independently created a detailed list of what we wanted in that partner. When we initially met each other, we discovered that we each had a 'want' list. My wife's list consisted of twenty-six items. My list consisted of twelve specific wants. We shared some good laughs comparing lists. One thing is for sure, we each had a goal written out, along with great specifics.

Do not be vague about what you want. A relationship partner? Describe them in detail. A new car? Write down exactly, specifically what you want. A new job? Describe it in writing. Make your thoughts very specific about exactly what your goal is.

Number 2: Create your plan to achieve what you want. Whether it is work-related, health-related, money-related, or relationship-related, what is your plan to achieve your goal? Again, be specific. For example, when I decided that I was going to climb Mt. Kilimanjaro, I needed to create a plan for getting myself physically ready for the trek. I knew I needed to increase my strength, endurance, and flexibility, as well as increasing my ability to be more comfortable about camping in medio-cre conditions. I created my detailed training plan nine months before my trip and then started taking action. Reaching the summit at over 19,000 feet was the culmination of Steps 1, 2, 3, and 4.

Let's say your goal is to find that special relationship with that special partner. You have specifically described, in Step 1, exactly what you want. Now, what is your plan? Are you going to join certain clubs or organizations, visit certain places, or even try an internet dating service? Create your action plan for today. It does not need to be your final plan. In fact, your plan can and will regularly change, but you need your action plan for today. Have fun with it!

Number 3: Once you have the plan, take specific action related to your personal time availability. When I decided to write this book, I set the goal and evaluated my plan, and now it is time to take action. As I write this chapter, it is 4:30 am. I have about one hour before I go to the gym and then head to my real job. Regardless of my goal and plan, if I do not take consistent action, this book will not get written.

If you are wanting to lose weight and you have implemented Steps 1 and 2, are you now taking consistent action? If you want that new career, are you taking consistent action toward getting it?

Being a dreamer about what you want is great and can be exhilarating. Being a dreamer without consistent action, however, is a formula for underachieving.

<u>Number 4: Become an emotional match to what you want.</u> As I said earlier, this step took me a while to learn. I previously believed that the above Steps 1, 2, and 3 would allow me to accomplish anything I wanted. I now realize I was missing this final Step 4. Similarities attract. You must feel similar emotions, striving to attain your goal, as you will feel when your goal has been reached.

Imagine the happiness and positive emotions you will experience when you reach your goal. Then use these same emotions as you go about putting your plan in motion.

No matter how much I plan and work on this book, if the planning and the work is not fun, exciting, provoking, etc., then the results will not be what I intend. Put another way, if you are looking for that perfect mate but spend a good deal of time depressed about your lack of a relationship, or jealous of those who already have one, or brood about failed relationships, then you are not an emotional positive match for what you want. If you want a happy ending, you must practice and learn to enjoy the "now" of your journey.

Does the athlete enjoy only the final outcome of his endeavor or does he enjoy the practice and the game leading up to the result? Does the musician enjoy practicing for the performance or the performance itself, or only the applause afterwards?

Our journey towards our goals is what life is all about. There is always a new goal and a new journey. Learning to enjoy ourselves and have fun along the way is key to living life and achieving whatever we want.

Here's another example: let's say you are trying to earn or attract more money into your life. If the thought of money upsets you, if the people who have money make you jealous, if you believe money may be the root of all evil etc., then believe me, the money will remain off in the distance, regardless of your goal, plan or actions. However, if your goal, plan and actions are filled with the fun and joyous anticipation of reaching your goals, then the probability of attainment increases dramatically.

I have trained and tutored many salespeople. In one instance, I recall an individual who had almost all of the tools to succeed. She worked hard, and had a plan and goal, but she never quite received the anticipated results. She was always angry: angry with the product, angry with other employees, angry with customers. She never learned to enjoy the journey and, for that reason, never achieved the desired results.

I have heard that the late Jim Valvano (college basketball coach), who I quote later in the book, actually had his players practice "cutting down the nets" during mid-season practices. This symbolized winning a championship. What fun, and what a feeling!

Okay, do you know what you want? Good. Set the goal. Make the plan. Take the action, and become an emotionally happy match with your journey. Practice that feeling of already having exactly what you want!!!

Now you've decided to put your four-step plan into action in order to get what you want. You are excited. You set your goal: how about losing weight? You make your action plan: diet with new food choices and exercise. You start to carry out the plan by avoiding fried food, reducing your caloric intake, and walking three miles per day. Lo and behold, you feel thinner, happier, and more energetic. Everything is set into motion for you to receive just what you want, and then, "BOOM," it happens.

At your weekly weigh-in, there is no weight loss. You cheated and had French fries and a soft drink with that hamburger last night. Oops, a road block! You feel like a failure and you feel like giving up ... SO WHAT! Who does <u>not</u> hit an occasional road block?

What successful athlete has not had disappointing results, at one time or another? Who, in a successful relationship, has not also had some unsuccessful relationships? What successful businessman has not experienced periodic failures?

A few years ago, my friends, Ron and Peggy, were taking their family on a vacation to Hawaii. They had been planning the trip for many months. As departure day grew near, the joyous anticipation of this dream-come-true vacation was increasing by the hour. They arrived at the very crowded airport only to find out that their flight had actually been scheduled to leave two hours earlier. Oops, a road block! They had missed their plane, and no other flights were currently available. Obviously, Ron and his family were devastated.

They had set a goal, made a plan, acted on the plan, were in a great state of mind … and now a road block. Sound familiar? Did they go home and give up? Of course not. They KNEW that, somehow, some way, they were going to Hawaii. After calling all of the airlines for other flights that day, they eventually found one and departed for Hawaii for that dream-come-true vacation. So what is my point?

Ron and his family knew they were going to Hawaii. The road block did not send them home. The dream of warm temperatures, hot sand between their toes, the sound of the ocean waves, and fabulous fresh-fruit cocktails on the beach was still the objective. They KNEW they were going to make it!!!

You have all heard success stories. Thomas Edison conducted 10,000 failed experiments before the light bulb worked. Colonel Sanders had his first business success with Kentucky Fried Chicken at the age of sixty-five, after numerous business disappointments. My first six months as a commercial real estate salesperson produced one sale and a commission of $2,000.

Everyone hits temporary roadblocks, whether they are superstars or people like you and me.

Road blocks are never permanent unless you believe they are. Know where you are going and create that image. Have the faith that you can do it! Do not turn back because of a French fry or a weigh-in. Embrace the road blocks, laugh at them, and play with them. You will reach your goal weight or your dream vacation, no matter what!

Your Inner Radar

Would it not be wonderful if we had an internal radar system which always kept us on course, regardless of what direction we tried to go?

You know what I mean. *Is this the right food for me? Is this the right job for me? Is it time to have children? Is this the right relationship? Should I rewrite this proposal? Should I tell my spouse? Are my daily time allocations correct?* The list is endless, is it not? Would it not be great to almost always know whether we are making the right decision for ourselves, actually having our own personal radar system keeping us on track?

Good news! You have it. You have always had it and, better yet, you will never lose it. YOUR PERSONAL RADAR IS YOUR EMOTIONAL SYSTEM. As I said earlier in the book, "We are here in this life experience to feel good and have joy in the present moment. That is our purpose." Here it is: WHENEVER WE FEEL GOOD, WE ARE ON THE RIGHT COURSE.

It sounds so simple and easy. Then what makes it difficult? The thing that makes this concept of a personal, emotional guidance system difficult for so many is the very fact that your personal radar system is just that, it is individually yours. It is not society's system. It is not religion's system. It is not your parent's system. IT IS YOUR RADAR SYSTEM, and for it to work, you must recognize the personal individuality of your radar. We are all deeply influenced by what someone else tells us is the right course. Ask yourself now, *Is it more important what my therapist says or what I individually feel? Is what my religion says more accurate than what I feel to be true? Is what my government says more accurate than what I feel to be right? Is what my wife says more accurate than what I know? Is what my parents and friends say wiser than what I feel?* It is all about you and YOUR RADAR. <u>If it feels good, you are on the right course</u>, <u>for YOU!</u>

The following story is an excellent example of this point. My first marriage broke up about ten years ago. Of course, I found myself going through the usual trauma and drama that goes with ending a twenty-year relationship. I decided, early on, to make the best of a difficult situation, so my despair quickly softened and I allowed much of the discomfort to pass. In a final attempt to salvage my marriage, my now-ex-wife and I decided to try professional counseling. I entered the counseling open-minded and in good spirits. I must admit that my radar was telling me that the breakup was probably best for me.

During one of the early counseling sessions, the therapist, after noting my general up-beat demeanor, suggested that I take off my rose-colored glasses and "work on feeling more pain." What he said felt terrible to me, but I actually took his "professional" advice and tried to be less happy and feel more pain, even though my radar was telling me that this was ridiculous. In time, I ignored his advice and went back to my "rose-colored glasses," but this is a classic example of a time when I did not follow MY emotional radar.

How about when you are seeking a new relationship partner and you meet someone who your friends and family think is perfect for you but, internally, the relationship does not feel right to you? Do you rely on friends and family, or do you rely on how YOU feel?

When seeking new employment options, do you go after those opportunities that society and family deem appropriate or do you pursue those jobs which make YOU feel good?

When I decided on a career in sales, my friends and family were far from unanimous in their support. Sales did not offer the guaranteed salary or prestige that many other professions may have. I had to decide what felt good to me. I learned to listen to my own radar.

You innately know what the best course is for you. Stop asking anyone else the answer concerning your course, or caring what anyone else thinks. Start noticing and trusting your personal radar. When some course of action feels bad, it is not right for you. It may be right for others but it is not right for you. When it feels good, you know it is right for you, and that is what living life is all about.

God and Religion

Do I believe in God? My answer is emphatically, YES! If I believe in God, then who or what is this thing that I emphatically believe in, and must it be called "God"?

God is the source and essence of everything and everybody. God is only love and joy and God is not outside of you and me, God IS you and me.

Want to know why good feels good and bad feels bad? It's simple. When we feel good, we are a match to God, to our soul, to our spirit. Conversely, when we feel bad, we are not a match. The internal radar that we spoke of earlier is our connection to God. When we follow our radar, we feel good, and we feel good because we are a match with our soul, our spirit or God.

The idea that God would ever punish us for anything is absurd to me. The idea that God requires us to do anything for his love is just as absurd. God-force is love and joy in the moment, in every moment, and the more we can feel the love and joy, the greater our connection. When we are connected, we feel good, and when we feel good, we are a match to everything we want.

I have been raised Jewish and I do love the "community" of the Jewish people and the closeness I feel to this community. Do I really believe that Jews are the only chosen people, or that a loving, joyous, forgiving God would actually choose one person or group over another? That just does not make sense to me. In fact, it does not make sense that God would ever be angered by anything or anybody, or that God would hold any kind of grudge, or that God needs to be apologized to. Let us not forget God is 'Unconditional Love.'

God is part of each and every one of us, all joyous, and when you are not a match to this, you are blocking out your God-force, which in turn inhibits you from getting what you want.

Do not worry about God loving you; that is a done deal. Just accept the love and go on. If it makes you feel good to be part of a religious organization, then do it. Remember, DO WHAT FEELS GOOD TO YOU. That is all that is important. Relax. Take a deep breath. God loves you, no matter what. You cannot and will not be punished for anything, ever. Just reach for your connection. How? By doing the thing that makes YOU feel good. It is the most God-like thing you can do.

Some may say that doing what feels good to you may be harmful to others. If this is so, then who do we make the judge? The only logical judge is you.

Look at the big social and political issues of our time: abortion, criminal incarcerations and punishment, military involvement, education, parental responsibility. The difference of opinion on these issues and others is enormous and, contrary to certain beliefs, there is not just one answer from God or Source or whatever you wish to call it.

The answers are ours individually, and we are supported by Source. We must have faith in ourselves and our beliefs.

If it feels good, you are aligned with Source energy.

Foreverness
Foreverness
Foreverness
Foreverness
Foreverness
Foreverness

It is said that the only two absolutes are death and taxes. In fact, some do not pay taxes, so, really, that leaves death as the only absolute. Why is it, then, that something so definite as death causes us such terrible concern? We know that physical death will absolutely, positively occur, so why all the sadness?

Only two answers come to mind; One, being fearful of the unknown, and Two, being concerned that death is a total ending.

I want you all to heave a deep sigh of relief. WE ARE ALL FOR-EVER. Is our physical body forever? NO, of course not, but our God-force, our spirit (call it what you want) is forever. So, where is the proof, you ask? If you, like me, believe in God or Source Energy, where is your proof of this existence? It is a knowing, an understanding, and a faith.

It is totally illogical to me that we could possibly only live for the speck of time we call a human life span. If we are forever, why do we have no knowledge or memory of any existence prior to our current lifetime? The answer is because we are here to live NOW, with no encumbrance from previous existences.

I know this can be a difficult concept to accept, even though we so want to believe it. I am sorry there is no proof positive. Do you believe in prayer? Do you believe in Life outside our Planet Earth? Did we once believe the world was flat? What is it about these questions? They all take faith!

In Marlo Morgan's book "Mutant Message Down Under," I read a most simple, profound statement: "Fear is the opposite of faith." Think about it: faith in yourself, faith in your plan, faith in source, faith in for-everness.

When you have faith, fear evaporates.

When fear evaporates, you become an emotional match for all you want.

Think for a moment of the God-force we spoke of in the previous chapter. How could this spirit, this love, ever end? IT CANNOT. We are forever. Our spirit goes on and on, an extension, a part of source-energy. Death is nothing more than a physical end and a re-entry into a non-physical world of nonjudgment, clarity, foreverness and love.

Once you stop fearing death and have the faith of your foreverness, you take a giant step toward being an emotional match to all you want and the eventual manifestation of your desires. We also realize that being forever means you are never done. How relaxing a thought is this? Furthermore, you know from experience that as soon as you finish one project, you always create a new one. It is never-ending, just like you. Now, that *is* a relief. Go take that sigh.

The News

I hope, by now, you have gotten my point that, in order to get what you want (usually a very good thing), you must be its emotional match. In other words, you must find a way to feel good now, even before you get what you want. (I will get specific about how to do this at the end of the book.) Good attracts good. If you are feeling bad, emotionally, you can forget about attracting good. With this said, let us go on.

It is early Monday morning in late October, 2004, as I am driving to work at my Denver office. I am leaving the mountains of Eagle County, west of Denver, and it is one of those perfect Colorado western mornings. As the sun rises, there is not a cloud to be seen and the sky is so clear, so dark blue that you may even call it purple. I am sipping on my morning cup of coffee, and Tchaikovsky is playing on the CD. I cannot possibly exaggerate to you how wonderful I feel. The sheer beauty of the morning, the warm coffee, the music, oh my! My mind is racing with positive, wonderful thoughts. I am totally, completely connected to my spirit, my God-force.

As I approach my office (the ride seemed timeless), I decide I would like to get a quick update on my favorite football team, the Denver Broncos, and their victory the previous afternoon. I turn off Tchaikovsky and push the radio button for the local Bronco station, tuning in to the 8:00 a.m. news. In forty-five seconds, I find out about the soldiers killed overseas, an attempted rape downtown, and the growth rate of a certain type of cancer. In a short forty-five seconds, my mood, my vibration, my connection to Source has been dramatically altered. I instantly feel colder and considerably less at peace. My free-wheeling stream of thought has been interrupted.

So, what is my point? If you truly want to feel good now, and attract what you want, it is difficult to consume a large portion of the national and international news. I understand the News Business is a for-profit enterprise, and apparently the more negative and startling the news may be, the more the news is watched and listened to.

Pay attention to how you feel when you partake of the negativity. Then change your focus to the positives in your life and feel the difference. You can do this by conscientiously changing your thoughts. With practice and a little effort, you can learn to do this quickly.

I have found that limiting my intake of news (radio, TV & newspaper) has greatly helped me maintain my day-to-day, positive demeanor, which in turn allows me to more regularly attract my desires. In fact, I do not know how a "news junkie" can possibly remain consistently happy.

One of my dear friends is a chiropractor named Dr. B. I really enjoy my friendship with Dr. B.; he is a kind, gentle being. Early last summer, when I visited him for a treatment, he informed me that he had just started a 'news fast.' He was fed up with the continual, obvious attempts to startle us with bad news. (Apparently we have told the news outlets that we will pay dearly for such negative, sensational news.) Dr. B is now prescribing just such a 'news fast' to his ill patients for their own well-being. Just try it. If you do not want to go cold turkey, try reducing your news consumption over time and see whether you feel a renewed emotional balance. The truth is, everyday, millions upon millions of people on our planet enjoy a wonderful life experience. The news teams search the globe to find that minute minority who are having a poor experience. You can, right now, decide whether you wish to ride their hyper-inflated illustration of a world in disarray. Yes, many people are having things not go so well today, but the OVERWHELM-ING majority of us are doing quite well, thank you. Let your individual emotional guidance system work on its own. Try not to let others manipulate your feelings and your point of attraction to what you want.

Mine!   It's all about me!

Mine!

Mine!

Mine!

Selfishness

Mine!   Mine!

Mine!

Mine!   Mine!

By now, you have gotten the message: being happy is what it is all about. It is your alignment with who you are. It is your source of power to attract anything you want.

So, if being happy is where it is at, and doing what makes YOU happy is where it is at, then where does selfishness come in? Your parents, your spouse or your friends may think you are selfish. When it is all about you being happy first, others start to lay the "selfish" label on you. But what is it really? Think about it for a moment. When others call you selfish, is it not really and simply (there's that word again) that you are doing what you want to do, and not what they selfishly want you to do? What makes anyone else the judge of what is right for you?

Being happy right now means doing what you want to do, right now. Stop letting anyone else define your "selfishness" by what they think you should be doing. If it makes you feel good to volunteer your time, then do it. If it makes you feel good to make a charitable donation, then do it. If it makes you feel good to coach the kid's soccer team, then do it. But, above all else, do it for your own enjoyment and not out of a feeling of obligation or selflessness.

Years ago, on this subject, I heard someone use the word "selfing." Selfing was defined as being personally selfish for your own private happiness and enjoyment, without regard to what anyone else says or feels. Somehow, I think "selfing" sounds much better than "selfish."

I know this whole discussion of selfishness is a difficult one. Between society, religion, friends and family, we have a lot of people telling us what they think we should be doing to make <u>them</u> happy. It's time to check in with your personal radar. It's not about what anyone else puts on you. It's <u>all</u> about what you feel. Practice and learn to ignore what the others selfishly want you to do. Listen to yourself. You cannot go wrong.

We are all familiar with the observations of the local and national news-commentary shows, freely expressing how they think others SHOULD be behaving; i.e. "The President should not be golfing," "Oprah should not be on vacation during this event," "the CEO should have attended that gathering," etc. Be it a celebrity or a member of the general public, no one is short on opinions about what they selfishly think another should be doing. Stop giving anyone the stage to influence you, and start doing what feels right for YOU!

There is no right or wrong thing to do, except by your own standards. Look around; we are all so very different. We differ in what we like to do and we differ in how we think.

As an example, what do we like to do in our free, non-working time? Is the answer to this question not incredibly varied? *Reading, listening to music, playing sports, watching sports, sleeping, visiting with friends or relatives, shopping, playing with our children, writing, drawing, camping,* etc. We are all different. You need not conform to anyone else's ideas of what is best for you.

How do you feel when you do something someone else wants you to do, that you do not wish to? Usually, not so good … and what does that tell you? You are not a match to your source, your soul, your God-force. Trust your emotional radar; you will be happier and you will receive much more of what you want.

Relationships

When I speak to people about issues in their lives, the big three almost always surface: relationships, health and money. That's not to say these are all there are, but certainly discussions on personal happiness seem to center around these three subjects.

Let me start by taking my usual short, simple look at relationships. Relationships come in many forms; children, spouses, siblings, parents, friends, work associates, and so on. For the moment, I am going to focus on the *significant other* or *spouse* relationship for making my point in this chapter, but most of these comments will also pertain to personal relationships as a whole.

1) First things first. How do you attract the partner of your dreams? If you have been absorbing this book, that should be an easy question by now. Step 1: Set your goal. My wife Julie and I both made detailed lists of what we wanted in a partner, before we ever met. A coincidence? Step 2: Make your plan to find the person. Step 3: Take action. And Step 4: Be an emotional match to what you want. (Is this starting to sound familiar?) If your thoughts and feelings are not in a place of truly believing and feeling that he or she is coming your way, then Steps 1, 2, and 3, above, just will not happen.

Once you have found your partner, how do you create the relationship and keep it thriving over any period of time?

No beating around the bush. IT IS NOT YOUR PARTNER'S RESPONSIBIITY TO MAKE YOU HAPPY OR VICE-VERSA. We have already thoroughly discussed the fact that it is your individual job.

What I find, in unfulfilled and deteriorating relationships, is that it usually comes down to what one person is doing that makes the other person feel unhappy or unfulfilled. Again, it is your responsibility to be happy and fulfilled, not your partner's responsibility. When my wife and I were contemplating our wedding vows, we semi-seriously joked that the vows would go something like this: "My dearest Julie, I promise to do everything I can do to be as happy as I can be, day in and day out, and I want you to do the same." No relationship can flourish without each individual selfishly and lovingly enjoying themselves first. It is only after achieving this self-joy that you can give it to another.

You cannot believe all the wonderful things you want to do for your partner when you love yourself first. It has to be. How can anyone who is filled with freedom, love and joy do anything else? I love making my partner happy! Bringing her flowers, bringing her coffee in bed, complimenting her endlessly; it is all an extension of my joy-in-self. As a partner wanting a loving joyous relationship, you must receive joy out of your partner's freedom to live their own joyous experience.

When we take traditional wedding vows, we make some promises which frankly may be difficult to keep. "Till death do us part" sounds like a loving commitment, but when you realize how we can change, frankly, it's a tough one to meet.

Both my wife and I had previous twenty-year marriages. Both our previous marriages produced wonderful children, lots of fun, and love, and really little to regret. Things just change. It is the natural order. When you get into a relationship, stop worrying about the future. Live in the joy of today and let things run their course.

My closing thought on this subject of relationships does go beyond just couples. Many problems arise when we think we know what the other is thinking. I am sure that we have all been through the circumstance where an argument or disagreement came to a happy ending and we then found out, through discussion, that what we thought was the root of the problem just was not the case. The following statement has helped me enormously in all of my relationships, not just with an individual partner. "WHATEVER YOU THINK ANOTHER PERSON IS THINKING, YOU ARE WRONG." You may be wrong by an inch or you may be wrong by a mile, but you can never know exactly what another is thinking. When you stop trying to know and stop reacting to what you think another is thinking, you will be shocked to find how much more peaceful your relationships become.

In a recent business situation with my mortgage company, a salesperson lost a sale because a supervising underwriter felt the loan did not meet guidelines. The salesperson was certain that his sale was turned down due to a personal dislike by the underwriter. I have come to know that the underwriter made every possible attempt at making exceptions to complete the transaction, but was just unable to do so. The underwriter did not share with the salesperson the effort made to approve the sale. The salesperson "thought" he knew what the underwriter was "thinking," jumped to a wrong conclusion, and left our company for no good reason. No doubt, we have all experienced a misunderstanding like this, or have been an observer of wrong conclusions. Remember, we are all different! Embrace the knowledge that you cannot accurately know what anyone else is thinking.

Relationships with friends, in the work place, or at home thrive when individual happiness comes first and partners stop believing they actually know what another is thinking.

Relationships, like all else in life, change. Sometimes they just run their course. We are individuals and we grow in different ways. It is time to appreciate that this individual growth is not only okay but is to be expected. We certainly do not see things in our fifties as we did in our twenties. Allow the changes that occur, enjoy the relationships right now, and make your joy paramount. You will be surprised at how enjoyable your relationships will become.

Health & Doctors

How important is your health to your overall happiness? How often do you talk about your health, the health of another, or health problems around the world?

Here's the next big question: How willing are you to trust your internal radar system when it comes to your health? Who would you trust more, yourself or the doctors?

I think, in general, that doctors are wonderful, but are they all-knowing? Is Eastern medicine considered different from Western medicine? Both have highly trained doctors, yet each looks at our medicine differently; i.e. the use of heat or cold on injuries, acupuncture, chiropractic, surgery, antibiotics, etc. The debate is never-ending. If you trust your doctor more than your own radar system, what makes you certain his way is right? If you get more than one opinion, and they differ, how can you know who is correct for you?

Being and staying healthy is a function of your thoughts. Are you going to let those thoughts be initiated and influenced by another (the doctor), or are you going to learn to trust that 'all-knowing, source-connected radar' which we all possess?

Last winter, toward the end of the ski season, I injured my knee. It was not nearly as serious as the torn ACL I suffered ten years earlier, but it was still an injury that kept me from skiing and playing tennis. I visited the doctor who had performed my ACL reconstruction years earlier and, after careful examination and an MRI, surgery was recommended. Please realize that I have tremendous respect for my doctor, Dr. K. He is experienced, skilled and passionate about his profession; in fact, he is everything I could hope for in a doctor. After careful analysis, he determined that surgery was required to repair my knee, and he wanted to schedule it immediately. I have no doubt whatsoever that he was recommending what he thought was best for my well-being.

As I left Dr. K.'s office after his diagnosis, I just did not feel right. My radar was telling me something different. My radar was telling me that surgery was not the right course, and I decided to postpone the surgery, at least for the moment. Long story short, I never had the surgery and, almost nine months later, I am completely healed, skiing and playing tennis with zero discomfort. I tried some alternative healing methods and, possibly, they worked. All I know for sure is that my radar told me not to rush into the surgery and it was correct. Learning to trust your personal, emotional radar in the face of scientific, skilled recommendation can be very difficult, but I assure you that your radar is always on target.

Another example of expert medical advice involves all the diets that seem to be offered up. In speaking recently with my dear friend, Dr. George, a family physician, he informed me that while half his patients thrive on a high-protein diet, the other half appears to struggle with it terribly. How can this be? Is it because we are all different, and what is right for one is not necessarily right for another? That is why we have our radar system, to lead us to the correct decision for ourselves and not for anyone else.

We have talked a lot already about how thought creates your experience. Indeed, that is a premise of this book. If you are starting to believe that this is actually possible, then what happens if you are told that at some point in your life you will have heart disease, because your parents or grandparents had heart disease? If that notion became one of your dominant thoughts; I assure you that it would become an actuality.

My wife, Julie, is an adopted child. She has no idea who her birth parents or grandparents are. She has no clue as to their medical history, and she loves it. She has no preconceived notions or thoughts guiding her towards ill health; it is all in her control. It is my firm belief that all the talk in recent years about illnesses being passed from generation to generation is mostly nothing more than a self-fulfilling prophecy of misguided thought. The scientific community should love that statement and, of course, they would point to all the evidence validating illnesses being passed generationally from family member to family member. It is always difficult to go against so-called "hard and fast" proof. You must decide whether to trust your own guidance system or not.

Do you want to be healthy now and into the future? Simply pay little attention to the ailments of your parents (as they do not pertain to you) and, after consulting with your doctor (if you must!!!), make your own decisions, based on your personal radar.

Think perfect health, feel perfect health, BE HEALTHY!!!

Children and Parenting

What do our children expect, need and want from us, and what do we expect, need and want from them?

Frankly, our children really do not expect a whole lot, other than love and support. They have the same radar guidance system that we, the parents, have, so stand back and let them develop. Is it unusual for them to want and feel things differently than we, the parents, do? Of course not; they are their own entity. As parents, we all have the tendency to push our children to do what we want, rather than what the child may wish to pursue. Now, why might that be?

Could it be that what the child becomes is, in reality, for many parents, a symbol of what they are? Ridiculous thought, yes, but often so true. As parents, does our straight 'A' student enhance our feeling of self? Does the great athlete child enhance our feeling of self? Does the popular child enhance our feeling of self? Does the attractive child enhance our feeling of self? And does the opposite decrease our self-esteem? Do we push our child a certain way to make them feel better or to make ourselves feel better? Whatever the answer, why don't we encourage them to use and develop their own guidance system?

Our job as parents should be to allow and encourage our children to move in the direction their guidance system points them. That is our primary parental job. What they become is not the parent's fault or the parent's design. How often do we see siblings with the same parental influence turn out completely different from each other? One child is a great student. One child is not so attractive. One child is less coordinated. One child is organized and another is not. If there is anything, as parents, that we know for sure, it is that our lasting effect on our children is somewhat limited. Remember, our children come forth with their own guidance system to express themselves the way they feel best. Let's help them find out what that is.

Several times, in recent months, I have heard the following statement offered. It goes something like this, "You know, as a mother, I can only be as happy as my least-happy child." Have you heard this one?

Talk about moving in the direction of your currently most dominant thought! If one of your most dominant thoughts is of your own personal unhappiness because of the state of mind of one of your children, where do you think you are headed?: Certainly not towards joy.

We all love and care about our children dearly, but regardless, if you want to be happy now, and you base your happiness on what is happening to someone else, I guarantee you are heading in the wrong direction. Please, please, love and support your children, but remember they are living THEIR life experience, and the amount of control you have over that is just not that great.

Some of you may remember the late Jimmy Valvano, best known as the head basketball coach at North Carolina State. He was a great motivator and a great speaker. One of his most inspirational talks was given to a group of top-performing insurance salesmen, and the subject was his father. In his speech, Jimmy talked of his own relentless drive to become a successful basketball coach, and of all the different places, jobs, victories and disappointments he had experienced. Throughout these lifelong experiences, his father was an unabashed supporter and confidant. Jimmy regularly called his father for comfort and advice, and his father's response for assistance and support was always the same. "My bags are packed to come to you. My bags are packed," is what his father always said. He was telling Jimmy, "I'm always here for you. I'm always here for support. I'm always on your side." I loved listening to this speech, many years ago, and I love the message today. Be there for your children, but try and let them decide what they want; encourage them to learn how to use their own radar guidance system.

My parents have been a perfect example for this. Whether it was my decision to leave New Jersey to attend college in Denver, leaving a salaried financial career for the insecurity of sales, going helicopter skiing in Canada, getting a divorce, or writing a book, my parents have always been the perfect support system, and their message has been consistent: "Follow your instincts. You have our love and support." What more could a child ever ask for? Would you have appreciated this from your parents? Then why not at least give your love and support to your children?

What is one of the greatest gifts our children can give to us? Just watch them in their early years. Watch the natural joy. Watch them play, their natural curiosity not yet tainted by parental and societal values. They arrive in life trusting solely in their innate guidance radar. It is only over time that that we, as parents, often teach them to ignore this wonderful guiding light they have. If we, as parents, would observe the sheer joy and excitement of our children, we would know that they are here to enjoy the present moment, something so many adults have forgotten how to do. As parents, we can all attest that our young children arrive with the inner faith, that joy-seeking in the moment, which is what life is all about. In fact, why don't we all, as adults, decide to be a bit more childlike? Ah, now. There is a thought that makes ME feel good. How simple. BE MORE CHILDLIKE.

Please rest in the knowledge that, with or without parents' nagging, our children, if encouraged to use their guidance system, will be just fine. Want to do them a favor? Explain the radar system to them, love them, support them and get out of their way. It is their life to live.

Forgiveness

Do you easily forgive others? More importantly, do you easily forgive yourself? Maybe, most importantly, is there ever anything to forgive?

Let's start off by remembering that we are ALL part of source energy, God. If this wonderful, loving God of ours is totally allowing and non-judgmental, then is there really anything that needs to be forgiven? In the purest sense, forgiveness is nothing more than allowing and acknowledging that everyone is entitled to be who they are, not what we think they should be.

More realistically, in day-to-day life we seem to get caught up in our inability to forgive others and ourselves. Tell me, what could possibly be more un-Godlike? Think about it for a moment. How upset and unforgiving are you about things you have done, recently or in your distant past: what you did to your body, what you did to your children or parents, what you did to individuals you do not even know personally? Please realize, it is over, we are not perfect, and we are forgiven. Yesterday is gone!

Individually, we have all done some things we wish we had not. There is a helpful saying that should assist you in getting over it. Since you are, indeed, forever, Abraham Hicks says, "You never get it done, and you never get it wrong." You always move forward and have more and more opportunities. Please, if you want to be happier, right now, forgive yourself for anything that you may not have done in the past the way you would actually do it now. It's the most God-like thing you can do.

When it comes to others, really let your God-self shine. Why not try, today, forgiving everyone for everything they have ever done to you. Forgive your parents, your bosses, your spouse, your friends, your government, other governments, etc. You do not need to embrace anyone you do not wish to, but you can forgive them and stop wasting energy (anger, jealousy, revenge) on emotions which are going to lead you away from the things you most want.

To allow everyone to be who they are is very freeing. We also call this unconditional love!

If you are beginning to understand that being happier and getting what you want requires an emotional match within you, then you realize the importance of forgiveness. Do not forgive for any other reason than selfishly helping yourself become happier and more fulfilled. Step 4, the emotional match, and forgiveness, they are all the same. Come on, give it a try. See how it feels.

It may not be easy, but it can be simple. Whether we are thinking of our parents, spouse, boss, friend, government; they all have their own personal radar, their agenda, their life. Allow them to be. Why not, starting today, decide you are actually going to emulate the very God-force within you? <u>Allow all</u>! Is this not a freeing thought?

SMILE!

Politics

I am relatively certain that the concept of being a professional politician never entered into the thought processes of our founding fathers in America. Being a representative of the people was deemed to be a sacrifice, and initially a sacrifice which did not pay very well.

Oh, how things have changed. Politics has become big business. The media attention, the power it bestows, and the compensation which can be earned all make politics a powerful influence in our daily lives.

In many cases, our elected officials, in order to maintain their positions, need to convince each of us that without their help and influence in government our lives would be overrun with 'danger, illness, poverty, etc. etc. etc'. It is an interesting game to observe: create victims, come to the victims' rescue, and get elected for your "triumphs."

It is no problem if you wish to play this political dance for personal fun and enjoyment. The problem occurs when you actually believe that someone other than yourself can and should take care of you. This thinking can only lead to a feeling of disempowerment and a victim's mind-set. Take a look at the political babble in our society. Who *isn't* being victimized according to someone? The elderly, children, women, any number of minority races, those with physical handicaps, those with mental handicaps, the poor, white middle-management in business, teenagers, super moms, and even soccer moms … The list goes on and on.

The more we give our attention to being a victim, the more of a victim we become. Remember, thought creates our reality. Being happy and getting what you want is a 'me' thing.

The only one who has power over you is that person in the mirror … YOU!

Please, keep your own power. Regardless of who your president, senator, or representative is, or the party they represent, your happiness, contentment, and safety is an individual choice.

Creating our joy and point of attraction is completely individual, and no political party can possibly take that away, despite the fact that they constantly want to convince us otherwise. Sure, you may not agree with what is going on around you politically, but should you allow it to overwhelm your personal sense of well-being?

If you want to play the politics game, great! Play for the same reason we all play any game … for fun! When you start to take it too seriously, and allow a politician or political party to control your joy or happiness, you have been sucked in. Remember, it is YOUR life, created by your thoughts and actions. Please do not allow anyone to convince you that an outside force can control your joy and desires.

We have talked about this already; it's SIMPLE. Use the methods we have covered, laugh aloud at our political scene, and take TOTAL control of your destiny. Enough said? Go ahead, watch a debate, laugh, and have some fun!

I have these four friends—Ron and John on the left, and Vic and Seth on the right. I am regularly copied on their biting sarcastic political email battles, which in most cases are hysterically funny. I love these guys, and they truly have fun playing the political game. They are indeed passionate about their respective views, but they understand that no one but themselves controls their day-to-day personal happiness. They enjoy the politics of the day without sabotaging their well-being.

Sports, Competition and Life

These next two chapters represent some of my core passions in life, and I am very excited about finally spilling my thoughts into this book.

Two of the things I enjoy doing the most are being a sales person and playing and watching sports. Let's start with sports and competition, and how they possibly relate to this book.

By now, you know that this book is all about joy in the present moment, and I receive a lot more joy from ESPN than from the nightly news. What I love about sports, whether as a participant or as a spectator, is how it mimics life. In sports, you train for your event, think about your event, study for your event, and then perform. Then, by golly, you sometimes lose or fail to reach your goal and somehow, just like life, you figure out that even these results can add to the fun.

Watch the pros. A great baseball player only gets a hit three out of ten times; a great basketball player misses half his shots; a great quarterback throws 40% incompletions; great golfers loose more tournaments than they win; and great mountain climbers often do not reach the summit. But they all seem to love what they do, and we love watching them. Think about it; this is life. In life, we have goals, we plan, we perform, and often the end result is not what we want at the moment, but it is not over. It just means that tomorrow is another opportunity to try again. Life, like sports, is an exercise in learning to enjoy the process, not just the end result.

I love to hike mountains, play tennis, golf and ski. I love the joy of training, mental preparation and performance. I do not reach the summit of all my peaks. I lose my share of tennis matches, my golf is a roller-coaster adventure and, when skiing, I fall and sometimes crash. Sound like life? In my earlier years, I had not yet learned how to love the journey of training and then not succeeding. Over time, I've come to understand that the joy of the journey is the key. Winning is just the added cherry on the sundae, which creates the next goal.

Let's look a little more closely at competition relative to life. Most of us face some form of competition regularly in life: competition in school, competition for a partner, competition on the job, etc. Learning to successfully and joyfully compete under pressure becomes a necessary life skill. How can I perform at my best during a major academic test? How can I perform successfully when I meet my dream partner? How can I perform best when I need to speak to a business group and make a presentation? Let me try and show you how I do it, and how I finally figured it out.

If you follow sports, you recognize that there is a difference in how even the most elite of athletes perform when the pressure is the greatest. What allows Derek Jeter, Joe Montana, Michael Jordan, Pete Sampras, and Tiger Woods to perform at the highest level, under great pressure? Sure, great ability helps, but most of these athletes have had competitors with similar abilities. What makes some of us perform better when it really counts, and how can you learn this skill in life?

Earlier in the book, I spoke of getting what you want in four steps. First, set the goal; second, make the plan; third, work the plan; and fourth, be an emotional match to the outcome. Here is how sports, life and this plan converged for me.

Over the past twenty years, I have played a lot of intermediate-level competitive tennis. Up until about five years ago, I lost more than my share of the very close matches. It always drove me crazy. Finally (there are many benefits to getting older and wiser), I discovered how to put

Step 4 into effect. For you non-tennis players, when you lose a very close match, it usually means you lost only a few key points at critical times; a mere two or three key strokes can make the difference in a two-hour match. What I finally learned is that, after Steps 1, 2 and 3, I did not have to do anything spectacular during these key points. All I had to do was execute the same shot under pressure that I practiced hundreds of times in a relaxed state. Once I applied this reality, I started winning most of my close matches.

I recently heard that the great golfer, Ernie Els, tries to think of his children when he finds himself in critical, tense, competitive moments. Why does he do this? He does it to be a relaxed, happy, emotional match to what he wants to achieve. Get it? Ernie has the plan, the goal, and the skill. It all comes down to being the emotional match.

So what did I do and what can you do in your pressured life moments?

First, remember during that interview or presentation, you just need to perform at the same level you do in a relaxed state. What I taught myself, in tennis, is that the more tense the moment, the bigger the point, the more people watching, the more I needed to get my THOUGHTS relaxed and off the subject at hand. I would think about walking on a beach with my wife, petting my dog, laughing at a *Seinfeld* episode, anything to create within me a relaxed, happy match to what I wanted to accomplish. Suddenly, in tight matches, I started making all the key pressure shots that I naturally made when the pressure was not on. What a great, joyous feeling, to put Step 4 into action and watch it work, over and over again.

You can simply learn to do the same thing in life, regardless of the task or event. Have your goal, make your plan, practice and rehearse, and THEN free your thoughts to be that happy, emotional match to exactly what you want. Try this. You will not believe the joyous results you will encounter.

$elling and Life

Upon graduating from the University of Denver in 1973, my first job was in the credit-card industry. After being a college student, any income seemed like a lot, but after a few years on this job, the idea of making real money became a priority. Being in my mid-twenties, I looked around the business world to see what professions would allow me the opportunity to greatly increase my income in the near future. I observed that some young engineers and attorneys were doing well, but I was educationally trained for neither.

What I did notice was that there was a great opportunity for income in sales; car sales, securities sales, real estate sales, etc., and age was no barrier. In the summer of 1977, I entered the profession of commercial real estate sales. I had the good fortune of meeting up with a gregarious Irishman named Bill Riley. Bill was my first sales trainer and he taught me the basics of selling, which go far beyond business-world applications.

From a strictly business standpoint, my career has centered on selling commercial real estate and selling money (mortgage lending). But the understanding and application of the basics of selling have assisted me immensely in day-to-day living.

This book is all about living 'simple happy' and getting what you want. Understanding the basics of sales will assist you in getting what you want, on a regular basis.

For a moment, think about all the times you are selling yourself in day-to-day life: finding a love relationship, keeping that relationship, getting a job, seeking service from a vendor of any sort, joining a group or organization, dealing with your kids and family, etc. The list is never-ending.

So what are the basics of simply getting what you want by selling yourself? To begin with, please understand that you cannot sell something to anyone who does not have an interest in buying. Of course, you can educate someone as to why they may wish to buy, but if you can't get them to *want* to buy, regardless of your skills, there will be no sale. If you want a relationship with someone who has no interest in you, forget it. If you want a job where the employer is not hiring, forget it. With this in mind, here are the basics of selling:

1. Understand, selling is a numbers game. No matter how good a communicator you may be, you will receive numerous "No Thank You's." You must keep pitching, with the understanding that a certain percentage will always say "yes." A "no" is not the end of the road. It's just a place along the journey.

2. Have an intelligent, well-prepared, practiced presentation. No short cuts! Create and practice, create and practice …

3. Ask for your order (what you want). No one can possibly say "yes" if they are not asked to buy. You are asking people every day to buy "you." Remember to ask for what you want.

4. The ever-important: be an emotional match. Before you reach your goal or complete your sale, know what it will feel like when success is reached. Now, put yourself in that emotional state beforehand, as if your goal had been achieved. In other words, be an emotional match along the journey for what you will feel like at the destination.

Let me give you two personal examples. First, after having been married for twenty years, being single again felt a bit strange to me. Finding a temporary or full-time partner was a new challenge, and one I had little experience in solving. I decided to rely on my own sales teaching. 1) It was a numbers game. I needed to make myself available through friends, personals, parties, business meetings, etc. 2) I needed a well-prepared presentation. Simple, just ask lots of questions and you can't go wrong. 3) Simple again. Just ask someone you like out for coffee or dinner and 4) be a match emotionally. Be sincere. Be empowered. Be trusting. Once I started putting these basics to work, I had a great six years of single life, and then the even better experience of finding Julie, my wife.

My second example involves finding business opportunities. As I write this book, my nine-year-old mortgage company is closing its doors, as market conditions have made us obsolete. The company had a great run and made a lot of money at times, but it ran its course. No hard feelings; it was a wonderful business and personal experience. As I look for new personal-business opportunities, it starts with 1) the numbers game. I have identified about twenty individuals and companies in my area of expertise (mortgage banking) and have approached them about joint opportunities. 2) I have an intelligent, well-prepared presentation of what I have to offer them and the mutual benefits. 3) I ask for the deal. Some say yes, others no; that's okay. And 4) I'm an emotional match for what I want. I am excited, enthusiastic, happy and optimistic. I can feel the next success, just around the corner.

These are my stories. You all have your own, of course. Learning to simply sell yourself is all about getting what you want.

Helpful Hints
and
Reminders

The sixty-second vacation

I have continually spoken of the importance of being that emotional match to what you want, feeling emotionally today the way you believe you will feel when your desire is achieved. But at times, in life, things happen which can throw our well-being off track. You know what I mean; an argument with your lover, a traffic jam at the wrong time, a disaster at work, an illness, a financial set back, etc. In order to regain your maximum points of attraction, you want to quickly return to emotional well-being. Of course, you often times will not go directly from extreme anger to bliss, but if you can start by simply feeling a little better, the rest will follow.

I have found personally that the sixty-second vacation is a wonderful way to quickly and gently improve your feeling of well-being. We all have a favorite relaxing place, whether real or imagined; the beach in Hawaii, the fireplace at home, the mountainside full of wildflowers, etc. When you need a quick emotional lift, take sixty seconds and just put yourself there. Here is what I did recently. A lot of my stress may occur at the work place. I am an avid snow skier. Last year, my brother, Jonathan, mailed me a five-foot by two-foot poster of the famous back bowls at Vail, Colorado, which I have skied for over thirty years. I framed this five-foot-long poster and mounted it on the wall directly in front of my desk. Whenever I feel the discomfort of work-place stress, I take my sixty seconds and place myself right in the poster, gliding through on an imaginary two feet of fresh powder snow. Trust me, sixty seconds and I'm feeling totally different. Try this easy exercise. It's simple and I love it.

Unconditional nonjudgment

Throughout this book, I have spoken of this subject several times. Please, please, try to remember just how different we all are, and how different our likes and dislikes are. Why not try deciding today that these differences are just fine with you, and start practicing complete, nonjudgmental allowance of everything and everybody? If someone else's life is not your deal, simply let it go. If there are segments of this book which you think are either wrong or misguided, just ignore them. Learn to love contrast. Contrast is precisely what often identifies and inspires you to do what you want.

Other people's thoughts

Here is my statement to you again, and I feel it is worth repeating: "Whatever you think other people are thinking, you are wrong!" You may be wrong by an inch or you may be wrong by a mile, but you are wrong. I have noticed that much disagreement and upset comes from what we *think* others are thinking; our boss, our significant other, our parents and our friends. Please realize how different we all are, and how impossible it is to know exactly what anyone could possibly be thinking. Please stop letting your sense of well-being hinge on what you believe is in the mind of another person.

"When the student is ready ... "

You know the saying, "When the student is ready, the teacher will appear," right? Well, if you have made it this far in the book, there is information here that appeals to you. If you desire to share some of this information, I want to encourage you to be gentle about it. You came to this material because you were ready. If someone else is ready, great, but do not force it.

After many years of my own life, "Napkin Notes," "mutant messages," "Denis Waitely," and "Abraham/Hicks," all came to me because I, the student, was ready!

At another time and place, I might very well have been blind to it all. Enjoy for yourself and share gently. Thank you.

Taking
Action ➤

By now you may be finding that some of this 'stuff' is starting to make sense, but you just do not know specifically how to get out of your rut and get started.

Therefore, I am going to give you a specific action plan to try out.

My simple plan on the next page is exactly what I do EVERY DAY of my life. Not just when I feel down or low. I mean 'every day.' I do not do it based on my feelings or wants on a specific day; I simply do it, every single day. Why?

Because, every day, I deserve to be happy and to get what I want.

Go for it!

My Action Plan

Simple Summary, Simple Action

1. **Smile each morning upon waking up**. This is easy enough. Just lie in bed and put a big, broad smile on your face the moment you wake up each day. This feels good and, as it relaxes you, your resistance to all you want fades away. Make this a daily habit.

2. **Take a moment each day to appreciate specifically all that you have**. I mean it. Be specific. Possible examples can be appreciating my home, my parents, my wife, my children, my health, my job, the food I enjoy, the weather, my car, my favorite TV program, the money I have, my friends, my intellect, my clothes, my body, my neighborhood, my insight ... Make up YOUR list and be appreciative every day. Go ahead, make your list. We all have many things to be appreciative of, no matter how small. Now take a moment and tell yourself how appreciative you are and mean it, every day.

3. **Take time each day to mentally create the specifics of that which you want that day, tomorrow, and in the future. Do this immediately after #2.** Let's break it down: a) Today, I want high energy, I want to find a great parking place for my 9:00 meeting, I want to close that sale, I want to have fun at work, I want to enjoy my conversation with my spouse, I want my body to feel good ... Easy enough? Just list what you want today. b) What do I want tomorrow and into the future? I want more money in my bank account, I want to be twenty pounds lighter, I want that specific

new car, I want that new house, I want that relationship, I want that job. Feeling better? This should be simple and FUN. Start your wish list of 'wants.'

4. **Try to avoid large doses of the news media**. Your choice here, but the combination of being a happy emotional match to what I want and watching or reading lots of news just does not work for me.

5. **Show unconditional allowance towards everything and everyone**. Remember, we are all different! Let it be! You will forevermore encounter individuals who do and say things you disagree with. Allow them to be who they are and, most importantly, you be who you are. You have no control over others, only over the way you react to them.

6. **Accept that you, your spirit, is forever. Your spirit will never die. You will never finish. You can never get it wrong.** We are not here to finish anything (because we are forever). As soon as we finish one goal, we want something new. It is the way we all are. We are here to do and to enjoy. Relax in this knowledge. There is no timetable.

7. **Make being as happy as possible, in the moment (right now), your ultimate goal.** How? By making it a goal, making a plan, taking action, and working on feeling a little better right now. What could be a simpler, more enjoyable goal!

Try the seven steps above, each day, for 30 days. Just see what develops. Try it. What do you have to lose, if you are not currently receiving the joy and manifestations you deserve? IT'S SIMPLE and it can be lots of fun.

Dear Friends,

Please remember what I said early in the book: we are all different. You are different from me. Your spouse is different, your children are different. Some or many of the things in this book may not be for you. See how they FEEL. Your radar will tell you what feels right for you.

It is said that a definition of insanity is doing the same thing again and again and expecting different results. If you are not getting what you want, and if your happiness in the moment is less than you deserve, think about a change. IF you preach Murphy's Law, are a "regular" at pity-parties, and thrive on the daily news, why not try something different?

Go on a sixty-second vacation. Pet your dog or get a massage. Do something right now to get your emotional vibration more in tune with what you want and who you are.

As this book comes to a close, my clarity is at an all-time high, and my "today" goals have been reached. If you have completed absorbing this book, I hope you have enjoyed the read as much as I have enjoyed writing it.

With Love and Appreciation,
Andy

Simple Happy Sources:

Dr. Denis Waitley

Napkin Notes on the Art of Living, by G. Michael Durst

Earl Nightingale

Abraham-Hicks Publications

Steven Covey

Mutant Message Down Under, by Marlo Morgan

Ramtha, J.Z. Knight

Jimmy Valvano

New 6 set CD

"SIMPLE HAPPY, THE NEXT STEP"

A lively, insightful, and timeless full length interview with Andy answering all your questions.

$97

includes:

-6 set CD-"Simple Happy, The Next Step"
-original book on CD (actually read by Andy)
-Andy's happiness planner
-Simple Happy baseball cap

GO TO WWW.SIMPLEHAPPY.NET

THE AUDIO BOOK ON CD

"SIMPLE HAPPY"

Finally learning to listen to yourself

Read by the author Andy Feld

$25.95

Go to:

WWW.SIMPLEHAPPY.NET

TO CONTACT ANDY

FOR SPEAKING ENGAGEMENTS

REGARDING LIFE SKILLS, SALES AND

INSPIRATION

Go to:

WWW.SIMPLEHAPPY.NET

<u>Notes:</u>

Notes:

<u>Notes:</u>

<u>Notes:</u>

This is Andy's first book. He grew up in northern New Jersey, moved west and graduated from the University of Denver in the early 70's. His business career began in Denver, but he has lived the past twenty-five years in Albuquerque, New Mexico. Just recently, Andy and his wife, Julie, moved back to the Denver area to pursue new business interests. Andy is available for speaking engagements regarding life skills, inspiration, and sales. You can reach him via email at andy@simplehappy.net

Notes:

978-0-595-43626-2
0-595-43626-9

Printed in the United States
100662LV00002B/103-111/A

9 780595 436262